Poetic Moments

Poetic Moments
Patricia Cruzan

Clear Creek Publishers
Fayetteville, GA

Patricia Cruzan, Author
Clear Creek Publishers
115 Clear Creek Court
Fayetteville, GA 30215-4642

My business e-mail address is cbusinesspat@aol.com.
Printed in the United States of America
Poetic Moments: poems/Patricia Cruzan

ISBN-13: 978-0-9653543-8-7
ISBN-10: 0-9653543-8-5

For all my friends and family

Other Poetry Books by Patricia Cruzan are listed below.

My Reflections
Sketches of Life

Patricia Cruzan's Children's Books

The Wonder in the Woods
Max Does It Again
Molly's Mischievous Dog
Tall Tales of the United States

Contents

Travels

Seasons and Nature

Great People of the Past

Life

Travels

Elvis Presley's Boyhood Home

A two-room ranch displays
rooms to sleep and to cook;
it meets the family's needs.

Shadowy cooking pots,
wooden chairs, a table, and a high
chair equip the kitchen.

Candles give light for tasks:
reading, writing, or walking, and
reaching outhouses.

Musical Beginnings for Elvis

Music in church provides
Elvis's introduction to
chords and group singing.

Others' influences aid
Elvis with chord formation,
quartet singing, and performance.

Teachers provide encouragement;
they help Elvis attain
fundamentals of music.

Elvis's rock and roll
evolve from blues, country, and
gospel music with movement.

Relics of the past
line Graceland and a garden:
Elvis reminders.

The Amish Way of Life

Women walk in with high-necked, long dresses;
faces lack makeup. Hats cover tresses.

Ladylike, thick dresses don't show much skin.
Everyone's outfit blends in with their kin.

Papa and Babe wear blue and black;
Babe goes shoeless. Dad's shoes are black.

Phone poles spiked hold spirited horses;
they wait to go on directed courses,

to lead their carriages here and there,
whether strong males or striking mares.

The Old Route 66 Restaurant

A restaurant's across from a museum;
it offers a variety of food:
Midwestern and Italian.
Vegetables and salads are beside
noodles, steaks, and fish.

Potatoes come laden with gravy, while
bread is an added delight.
Various drinks are there:
tea and carbonated ones.
Sweets complete the fare.

The Country Music Hall of Fame

Mahogany and steel guitars reside
beside black and tailor-made suits,
brown, fringy jackets, and sequined coats.
Horizontal pockets add trimming.
A frock with a slender waist and a full breast
rests beside beaded gowns.

A low-cut gown's there; it's nearly backless,
of taupe and orange, with varied lengths,
stays on with a string tie. Women's dresses
reflect fashion garments of yesteryear.
Vertical beads extend down the gown;
they attract eyes to the tall and lean look.

The photographs line the walls
of duos; they show fan notes and reminders,
and representation of gold
and silver records of performers' sales.
The records show accomplishment on and off stages,
in the United States of America in music.

A customizable car with fins
reflects an affinity for guns of old.
The front, sides, and trunk of the car
display the fascination with guns.
The dashboard continues the theme,
of a cowboy, surrounded with guns.

A gold Cadillac has style that stands out;
the seats and carpets look luxurious.
The fancy intercom system
allows conversation with the driver.
The headlights and the limousine
impress the tourists with the upgrades.

The Hotel Blues

Cheap hotels smell musky, moldy,
tainted, and foul. Carpets are shabby;
they reek of ground-in dirt from years.
Worn pieces connect the frayed pieces.
Dingy sinks spoil basins for washing;
handles need muscles to turn on or off.
Bathtub plugs don't seal.

Premium items like toiletries are missing.
Lumpy mattresses shift at night;
sea waves come in and out. The guests get
naps, when it's quiet, without noise.
People slam doors at midnight,
and voices talk all night; they increase
in volume at midnight and morning.

Intermediate hotels have beds
one can rest on, but showers fail;
stoppers don't hold, so water escapes.
Wi-Fi service works only in places
set aside by the permanent staff.
E-mails load at a snail's slow pace.
Linens are superabundant but vanish.

Patience is needed in hotel stays;
objects aren't right, or are missing from rooms.
Guests discover necessities are missing:
napkins, washcloths, and towels.
Premium prices are hard to pay, but
having viable things is so important.

The Boondocks Café and Motel

Farms line I-20;
stations aren't in sight.
If you need a break or rest,
plan for stops and breaks.

Tourists hunt some amusement;
jukeboxes play.
People chat for hours;
they play games and talk.

A State of Silos: Iowa

Tourists travel miles and miles;
they observe tillable soil about.
Soil contrasts with tiny shoots;
the dirt of earth grows fertile crops.
Farmers place nutrients for healthy plants.

Silos span for miles all around;
they keep crops fresh, and in storage till purchase.
Farms have buffer bushes that rise;
buffer bushes keep soil in place.
Dirt remains close to the plants.

Brick-red barns crop up all over.
The moving soil contrasts to roofs.
Glossy rays gleam through azure skies.
Clouds become puffed vapor masses;
when inflated, limpid drops fall.

Aloha to Honolulu

Honolulu
welcomes with warm, deep water.
Grass skirts and colorful orchids
pull in eyes on beaches.
Vibrant suits and muumuus
add color to Hawaiian girls.
Hues are added with a lei.
The swing of hips attracts
those who move to the rhythm,
who represent mixed cultures.
Pineapples flavor,
whatever one eats in Hawaii.

The Hawaiian Restaurant in Georgia

The unique restaurant with the hut corner
has thick, wooden logs supporting grass strips.
The birthday table shines;
it seats ten to twelve small patrons for events.
The guests await the celebration.

Pineapple on bacon burgers
give customers a mouthwatering taste.
Macadamia nut shakes taste different,
along with pineapple slices.
They make the restaurant a special eatery.

The middle partition inside supports
a gigantic planter filled with plants:
purple, yellow, and orange flowers.
Waxy, green foliage is a backdrop
for nature's eye-catching colors.

A webcam depicts sea views
of the time zones and sandy beaches.
Off the foyer are wooden stalls.
The wooden floors hold attractive sinks:
green, flat slabs with darker flecks.

A Retrospective City

The capital city beckons
with eye-catching appeal.
For what city offers so much
to the mind's imagination?
A lengthy and reflective pool
stands between strong monuments.
One marvels at the men's construction,
of the artisans' time and work.
Seekers search for the men
who helped set up democracy
in America years, ago.

Tourists seek out attractions
by Pennsylvania Avenue.
The President's grand, columned house
welcomes visitors here.
The splendid, historical rooms
capture visitors' eyes.
The furnishings of years gone by
help the tourist see
homes of yesteryear.

A Charming City

Paris, a graceful and elegant city,
combines a charm of the old and the new.
Notre Dame has Gothic towers,
and a stained-glass sanctuary, that
dates to many centuries ago.

The Louvre's modern-glass pyramid
stands in stark contrast to the art,
adjoining the cathedral's corridors and rooms,
built by the king's craftsmen for a church.
At Versailles, fountains, gardens, and lakes
surround the tourists with lovely scenes.
Inside, opulent and inviting furnishings,
carved woodwork, and paintings intrigue.

Romantic strolls along the Seine,
combine with flower market stands,
to create settings for love to bloom
if you see your fellow in Paris.
Latin Quarter and café excursions
provide images of skillful craftsmen;
the artists create and sell their wares,
with the grandeur of the Eiffel behind them.

An Imposing Building

Monuments and capital buildings
furnish architecture,
and factual, historical accounts
of people's lives in stone,
or plaques of commemorative events.

Nineteen feet of a figure
stands by thirty-six blocks.
Massive columns adorn
the memorial with Lincoln's statue;
the effigy faces east.

Think of Georgia's state capital:
an edifice in Atlanta.
Limestone surfaces,
while Georgia marble, pine,
and iron ore adorn the inside.

Bronze statesmen statues and markers
add to the building's bricks
from the old city hall.
Magnolias, elms, and oaks
line the landscape.

Seasons and Nature

Winter's Vengeance

The weather has a high of sixty degrees
until the howling winds do blow.
Temperatures drop down so low
into the teens, and even below.

Wind chill makes it freezing, as though, it's
ten degrees with needles which prick
red, bare skin while one's out to kick,
snow through the frozen and hard ground.

Hair flops all around in wind
on a crochet and colorful cap;
wind keeps pounding the cap like a rap.
Pedals power against resistance.

Trees yo-yo in and around in the breeze.
Ice stays frozen in open spaces;
it looks like colored diamonds on laces.
Ice sticks to the bumpy trunks.

Bikers' faces turn cold and crimson;
biting gusts come from wind's fierce gale.
The gusts whip over each hill and dale.
Then electric flames shoot fire out.

Winter

Old Man Winter sends
trees that shake and bend.
Laden down with the snow,
branches bend so low.

Winter brings snow for peers;
children send out cheers.
"Let's build a snowman," they say,
while they toss snow away.

Kids take snow for a ball;
they are careful, so it won't fall.
Once it remains in place,
the ball becomes the base.

Kids grab another ball;
it forms and gets so tall.
Kids' shoes move with a crunch
as they scurry home for lunch.

Snow goes up for a top;
it's put up, so it won't drop.
After this ball is its head,
it gets a scarf of red.

Rock eyes go in so tight.
The nose starts to gleam in light.
The mouth attracts those around,
but from it there comes no sound.

Nipping Days

The wind blasts miles of air;
it seeps through heavy socks.
Pinched toes reside in shoes,
afraid to leave their home.

Leggings, pants, and layers
resist the nipping wind.
The wind pierces downward;
it penetrates the clothes.

The vicious waves of air
rip through a fuzzy hood;
the freezing weather hurts;
the hood stops cold pockets.

The wind's bitterness stings,
and numbs knobby noses.
Eyes steer one ahead;
they hold moist droplets.

Lips tremble back and forth;
they sing well-known verses.
During winter's wind,
people search for warmth.

A Southern Gentleman

Snow moves, blowing as white flowers;
flakes tumble, falling in showers.
Thick flakes coat as they abound.
Snow falls gently, without a sound.

Various shapes, they're not alike.
The flakes swirl, and drop on each tyke.
Boys run; they have balls to throw.
Balls fall to the vast plateau.

Frozen crystals blanket the ground.
Children roll ice, for the first mound.
Kids make a ball; a second one forms.
They throw ones toward college dorms.

Another ball goes on the top.
When the head is made, one works nonstop,
making eyes, a nose, and a mouth.
Kids shape a man from the south.

The Whispery Winds

On a wintry day, the sun fades.
In trees, a sound comes from some blades.
Kids go to a sleigh. Elf speaks,
"Come young children to a safe place,
where real dreams come true to seek."

Santa's full pack brings out a cheer.
Kids see kindness, from a small deer.
They give presents on Christmas night.
The children say, "Thanks, Santa Claus.
We see the sleigh. It's quite a sight."

A Chance Meeting

Three whitetail deer graze flora;
two leap away from one.
The lone deer's ears hold firm;
it doesn't run away.
Does distance keep it placid?
A soft voice calms its fears.

A tapping engine sends
it to the sylvan setting.
The panoramic vista
shows off its dapple coat,
against the empyrean sky
as lustrous moon ascends.

Perceptions

Leaves of orange, red, and brown
crackle underneath one's feet;
they send sundry music out,
if we listen for the beat.

Leaves hang loosely on the tree
till the winter winds gust forth;
flying leaves go here and there.
They go aground or fly north.

Naked branches on trunks stand tall,
lines against a robin's egg sky.
Tree trunks stand, a contrast to the blue;
once they bloom, humans just sigh.

Spring brings lots of blossoms and hues:
pastel pink, dark purple, and pear.
Blossoms bloom all throughout the spring;
they make a lovely summer's fair.

Dog's Reactions

Jay sits near his master;
he sits extremely close.
He rests on his haunches;
Jay doesn't show morose.

He runs far to the right;
the dog avoids the device.
Gadgets injure the ears;
they're not meant to entice

one beside the gadget.
Jay responds to loving
strokes and pats from humans;
he doesn't want shoving.

When the contraption stops,
Jay sits and relaxes;
the eyes begin to shut.
Master works on taxes.

Summertime

Southern and sultry summer days
heat up bodies sitting still.
Buzzing bodies search for pollen;
blinking lights give winks to all.

Playmates come from peers;
they dance by the beige and sandy shore.
Sweat drops fade after ocean dips.
Lemon balls fly on every side.

Fishing poles line nut-brown piers;
people reel fish for Mom's fish fry.
Buckets contain the daily catch;
small, scaly fish fill up the brim.

Ocean trips present a symphony.
Timpani beat the shining shore.
Flutes hiss clear and charming tunes;
water coughs small hermit crabs.

Tourists move out on sandy feet.
Salty mats show off their crystals.
Scarlet bodies stroll to showers;
bodies rinse specks of pure diamonds.

Rays of Sunlight

Tallish flowers of gold
stand knee-high;
the plants bring the sun's rays.

Brilliant and immense petals
contrast to coffee eyes,
and seeds supply nutrition.

Rain at Dusk

Chilly wind brings rain—
sprinkles bedew cars.
Rainbow raincoats grace
tiny, tenebrous figures,
staying clear of flowing rills.

A Nature Walk

Calm moments
call us to bask in
the allure
before us—
flower silhouettes and ducks
sway ceaselessly here.

Spring Brings

Easter crosses
chocolate eggs
spongy ducks
golden mist
gentle breezes
radiant blossoms
emerald trees
blissful days
cottony clouds
clear, blue skies
grasslike blankets
picnic trips
long days.

Love blooms
birds cheep
animals mate
kites soar
glowworms fly
bugs flash
owls hoot
grasshoppers chirp
mantises pray.

Spring Thoughts

Spring brings thoughts of gentle breezes.
Yellow mist descends all around.
Vivid blooms toss on windy days.
Love blossoms out on blissful days.

Verdant trees reach skyward to clouds;
fluffy clouds drift in varied shapes.
One discovers friends who relax;
friends open special surprises.

Birds sing charming trills for partners;
calls to mate go out in woods.
Kites ascend and fly in skies.
Glowworm lights flick on at dusk.

Grasshoppers chirp in fields.
Owls make hoots in trees of brown.
Crickets chirp out rhythmic sounds.
Mantises pray in black trees.

Think of the Via Dolorosa;
Jesus displays a bruised body;
He suffers the floggings of cruel men.
Jesus offers redemption from hell.

Nature's Sounds and Sights

People rise in the morning,
to glimpse nature around.
Beauty arrives in seasons.

Fall has colorful leaves;
winter brings lacy flakes.
Spring has striking flowers;
summer brings seashore fun.

Stop to view the beauty—
hues of varied colors.
Relish the eye appeal.

Leaves hang loosely on trees
until winds start blowing.
Then, they fall to the ground.

Bare trunks tower skyward,
nude silhouettes till spring.
Blossoms sing so softly;
blooms show off their shapes.

The Magnolia Tree

Standing taller than five, tall men,
the tree makes it through nature's storms.
The trunk spreads out to fifty inches,
and supports the tree's lofty branches,
that spread out skyward, for all, to see.

Three-inch, fragrant flowers add smells
to rooms, and furnish a fine view.
The sturdy petals become quite bruised,
as a bicyclist's knees do after a person
missteps on one of the pedals that move,
and sends one down to the ground's surface.

A rope swing, which hangs from a bough,
invites the child in all of us
to push, relax, and enjoy the ride,
as it winds down, to feel the wind
upon the head, arms, trunk, and legs;
it reminds us of past merry-go-rounds.

Spring in the Air

The birds' enchanting songs stir me in spring,
and pollen coats my street, walk, and car.
I stop to think of what my day will bring,
while I gaze at hanging limbs I see from afar.

The sunlight casts its beams through panes;
the sun invites me out to feel its heat,
to wonder off through meadows, fields, and lanes,
or just relax outside, to take a seat.

I feel the gentle breeze caress my skin,
and sweep the grass and leaves from side to side;
then spread the different seeds on my chin,
and with them drift away to glide and hide.

I turn again to hear a bird call out,
while mother bird sings and flitters about.

Beauty

Blooms
grow
colored,
bold or pale,
in mixed sizes:
slight versus gigantic stems.
Deep, colored plants show shadowy parts, dancing wildly.

Oh, the Place to Go

The waterfall flows from a river
over lands; it gives a peacefulness.
The fall snakes around all over and under;
it creates a natural kind of beauty
a painter, or artist can never capture
in a drawing, or composition of art.

Our God formed different works of beauty.
He speaks through art, which tell of His greatness,
and what's in store for man in His world.
Places can be restful, or noisy for people;
they can meditate, or enjoy the beauty,
as one goes about for playgrounds.

The flower blossoms
with frocks of Chantilly lace;
it showers petals.

Rain

Rumblings break the eerie silence.
Streaks of light form shapes of cover;
thunder resounds in the downpour.
Rain gushes out from house drain spouts.

The rain halts as if by magical power.
The pins and needles pound the house;
they spill on the roof, the door, and the window.
Interval flashes break the blackness.

A glimpse of the morning light begins;
the hazy, gray light illumines the sky.
Bedroom windows show scenic images.
Tapping sounds descend from the gutters.

The rain slows down; then it pelts again.
An emptiness remains in the house.
Yards still stand; they're mired in mud.
No invitation comes to enter.

Muddy feet make dog paw tracks;
reddish-brown carpet tracks remain.
The storm begins to disappear,
but inside one hears the rain come down.

A Summer Visitor

Eyes watch to open the gate;
the orbs observe for creatures:
insects, spiders, or lizards.

A sea-green reptile's frozen;
it's on a bottom, small twig.
A being stands close in proximity.

A person startles and alarms,
when he lifts the fence latch slowly.
The reptile goes leaping downward;

it causes a deafening scream.
The reptile dashes from paws,
too massive and close for comfort.

Still as a Statue

Deer stand still at dusk,
statues with milk-white tails.
Deer are buff and ivory.

Sounds can produce running;
they cause immediate action.
Legs leap off to woodlands.

One Little Leaf

A leaf tosses and yells,
"Come out and play with me.
I have no friends for play.
I wonder where they can be."

"I'm waiting for my friends;
the wait is very long.
My friends will come along,
once bird sings out his song."

"My friends can help me on,
because I'm tired from knocks.
They send me everywhere.
I must find strength like rocks."

The Miracle Crop

The "goober pea's" nutritional;
it has some 300 uses.
As wonder crop, it gives
food and provides a living.

Some parts appear in glue,
cooking oil, and rubber.
At times, the wonder crop
emerges in nitroglycerine.

Ball games and circuses
offer the "goober peas."
Lookers-on enjoy it,
along with one's attraction.

Mr. George Washington Carver
sees the crop's potential,
before the crop becomes
the marvel of nature it is.

The Ruckus

The rowdy bark awakens,
and startles those in slumber;
there's something amiss in the yard.
Eyes close from loss of sleep.
The owners view the lights
from streetlights' rays that dance,
on hoods of cars and trunks.

The drowsy eyes see nothing,
while looking through the blind.
The cars, a silver Fusion
and red one, sit still.
No person sits near.
The noise continues until
the sleeper's eyes pop open.

The morning sounds begin:
a microwave comes on.
The dishes clang together
and water streams down sinks.
Garage doors open and close.
Sleep comes to an end
from the telephone's ring.

The couple glimpses out,
to see the trash abandoned.
The man spots the garbage;
rubbish is everywhere.
The man sees trash all over.
The view shows messy paper;
the paper disappears.

The Signal

Whenever the dog barks,
it's a call to action.
Visitors wait at the door,
or critters in the yard.

Frantic digging and barking
signal something is amiss.
The sanctuary is silent;
it becomes a playground.

The playground is noisy;
one seeks out the reason.
A person walks to see;
a paw begins to slap.

An open gate reveals
a slithery snake goes by.
It coils around to strike;
it dangles from a mouth.

A shovel sends the creature
back to the wooded regions,
out of the dog's quick snare;
the snake returns to its home.

Irresistible

With my best stance, my head held high,
I flash my large and longing eyes;
I yearn for love from my best friend.

With a wishful look, I'll show my coat;
my coat glints gold against the sky.
My friend's voice mollifies my fears.

With a foremost paw, I clear my eyes,
and lick away the mud and grime,
to keep my master petting me.

My tail speaks volumes as it wags;
the motion takes the place of words,
so my master will stall as he turns.

My hanging tongue works fast you see,
to plant my kisses here and there,
so master will stay awhile to play.

I know if I can keep him here,
to give him lots of looks and signs,
my man will find me irresistible.

The Sun

Snow clouds vanish;
they're not tannish.

Snow starts to melt
from last night's pelt.

Sun casts its spell;
it's sky's deep well.

Sun's aging mare
leaps from where?

Sun tricks earth's guests;
it evanesces.

What Is Ahead?

Burnt orange, yellow,
and russet leaves
line the serpentine way.

Leaves on the left
face glossy, green ferns and
arrow-shaped pines.

Verdant meadows
welcome us
to nature's blanket.

Meadows invite
the tranquility
of the moment.

What's beyond the trail?
Waterfalls or woods,
which teem with floras and faunas.

Do streams flow,
giving a restoration
to the soul?

The weathered path
has delightful sights
and captivating songs.

Great People of the Past

Sparks of Genius

The fireworks start: a stateroom
fills with brilliant minds. C. S. Lewis,
Haydn, Handel, Schubert, Bach, and Nash,
Armstrong, Newton, Blake, and Bohr come next.
Van Gogh, Picasso, Plato and Xenophon.

The minds fire at high-speed rates;
animated brains construct theories.
Some minds bring concepts all together as one;
they tweak a great deal of misinformation first,
while recording patterns likely found to exist.

Men of wisdom launch designs for products;
intelligent men improve their lives and people's.
Smart men harness power for electricity;
they forfeit arts for existence and man's wants:
music, writing, books, painting, and art.

Smart minds can create tasteful textures in music;
they can record sounds and weave their chords
of harmony and dissonance for everyone to hear.
Artists choose their mediums in artwork,
which attract the watchful eye of the person looking.

The literary world admires their work;
they entice readers with new meanings and different plots.
The writers entice their readers with details and points:
implied or explicit details are there to receive.
They send creative genius sparks to all.

A Leader for the Times

Our heritage begins with a strong man,
who serves other people, as he can.
Whether he sleeps on a bed or a cot,
Washington serves in a commanding slot.

He stays with his men while he sees defeat,
but shivers and fights, without much to eat;
he stands, a giant, while he faces despair,
with soldiers' uniforms that leave limbs bare.

When all is lost, he continues to fight;
his inner voice tells him what is right.
His men still win the war at last,
while they fight in a country, so vast.

The colonies retreat with freedom won;
they set the stage of what's to be done.
George's opinions carry much weight.
So, with his plans, there's seldom a debate.

An entourage of well-chosen men,
along with paper and strokes of a pen,
map out and set up a government plan,
for America to run, for a span.

He leads when needed, and steps aside;
he keeps his ego in check, not pride.
He's a man of absolute power;
George isn't scared of a wig with powder.

A Diplomatic American

Ben Franklin, of simple means,
seeks out a high life station.
By talking and dining with kings,
he gets a good reputation.

At age forty-two, he retires;
he leaves his trade as journeyman.
Franklin has offices around;
he's a distinguished gentleman.

He directs in a royal slot,
as deputy postmaster.
Vacillating ways help Ben;
they seem like such a disaster.

He serves as a diplomat;
he's one to emulate.
As men put down nobility,
his teachings resonate.

When he returns to his country,
his countrymen learn of his name;
they know not about his acts,
but wonder about his fame.

Life

A New Year

A wedding party assembles.
The ushers escort in guests,
with groomsmen in their positions,
in suits and ties of sable.
Bridesmaids wear lavender.
Observers utter, "Stunning."

Melodic music sounds forth
from the pitch-black piano.
The bride glides forward softy;
she glows with a flawless skin.
Her face has a fingertip
tulle veil with small disks.

Taffeta white tiers
stretch from the bridal gown.
Thin hands hold a Bible;
it's white with tiny pearls.
Inside the lacy Bible,
a blue ribbon adds color.

Joyful moments draw near:
music, vows, and Scripture.
Artists find great pleasure;
they share surprising pieces,
and talk of art impressions.
Art finds its final place.

Abiding Love

I love the trips you make each day and night;
the trips you make for viands at the stores.
The chores you do when I'm at my site;
I correct poems while you cut apple cores.

I love your thoughts and time for each small task.
I love the words you speak in love to friends.
I love your work, not clothed under a mask,
but deeds and words that don't prick like a pin.

I value times when you don't hang on me.
You disappear, so I can shop alone.
And I don't feel your eyes that stare and see,
the gift I want to give as your new phone.

I love your cheery smiles and laughter, too,
that come from joyful moments I'm with you.

Building a Life

Building a life means—
living triumphs and defeats.
Learn from bad mistakes.
Refocus on poor visions.
Revise your plans constantly,
never leave fine dreams.

The Wheel of Life

The wheel of life rolls
throughout all seasons.
For some, the spokes go fast.
They move like a rocket.
For others, the wheel grinds,
it plods along each day.

Events can cluster.
The wheel starts to spin,
until one day it starts,
to race again swiftly.
It never slows to the ground,
to enjoy God's creation.

At times, the wheel gets stuck;
it fights a strong resistance,
until it gets some leverage,
to pull it up again,
out from the murky water,
to turn to the right again.

God set earth in motion.
He gives man some choices,
to speed or slow his wheel.
Man's inner voice suggests,
decisions to be made,
which affect the wheel's pace.

A Mother's Love

Mothers extend their love to children
during birth, first years, and teen years.
After birth, mothers hold babies;
they cuddle and hug them to express their love.
Skills advance through years of practice,
once the youngster leaves his kin.

Mothers often miss their first triumphs;
coos, laughter, and smiles don't come.
They miss the other benchmarks.
Other children's births won't replace
bonds lost by death, for the one no
longer alive and present with them.

Puppies mimic humans; they stay by
moms through their meal and care daily.
A puppy's death will keep a mother
beside the child throughout her grief.
They stay through days, weeks, or months.
A mom never leaves the child for food.

Mothers and children stay in touch:
letters, visits, notes, and phone calls.
Kin continue with talks until
death puts an end to the friendly chats.
Moms look forward to life anew.
Hopefully, loved ones and kin will meet.

Many Hats

Which hat am I wearing right now?
My hats shift around all the time;
for hurdles, may alter my schemes,
with changes about me each day.

Adjustments are made through the week,
and hats may change in scope,
to wife, to mother, to sister,
to teacher, to cook, to learner,
to writer as part of my life.

My juggle starts at dawn,
when sudden things occur.
I place my child in his crib
and grab supplies for the day.
With diapers and tools of my trade,
I'm off to pack my car;
I leave the door ajar.

With care, I take my child,
my wondrous bundle of joy.
With blankets, I swaddle him,
to keep him warm from wind.
But then he cries again;
a diaper dries his tears.
I strap him in his seat.
I hope to get him by five.

My hat shifts to a teacher's;
I prepare lessons quickly.
The fire bell sounds; bodies
move to the fire exit,
to spots away from danger.
I watch as kids line up.

The bell sends out a signal,
to walk inside in silence,
and daily learning continues.
With a teacher's commanding voice,
I settle kids down to work;
I will not my duty shirk.

When planning is done for the day,
my hats shift on and off.
I grab my other hats,
as I have things to do.
I hurry along each day.
My hat shifts on when needed,
to soothe the hurts and cook.

The sister's hat comes on
to have a friendly chat.
So, family ties are bound,
and love can be rekindled.
In the evening my hat,
becomes a writer on the computer,
and I can plan plots,
to visit throughout the day.

What Do Mothers Do?

Mothers give care;
they serve as teachers
and moral models.
They entertain and
do house duties:
wash and chauffeur,
cook and dust,
sweep and scrub.

Moms show feelings:
laughter and tears.
They display their love.
Mothers are strong;
they give life's best.
Moms teach joy,
and attainable ways
of reaching goals.

Moms teach lessons:
biblical, social,
personal care,
and academic.
They're not infallible,
but plug away
through pain and sorrow.
They're good examples.

Foundations are set
for life, each day.
Moms model how
to work along
with others, or by
themselves. They're captains
of immense ships
who give out love.

Dancing

I'm anxious to go out,
and swing my legs about.

I'm active days and nights,
as I take in the sights.

I want to dance with friends,
and make some twirls and bends.

My kin won't let me dance,
but I just want to prance.

Listening to Music

A saxophonist blows
a downtempo blues
on French, grassy meadows.

A young trumpeter maestro
begins a melody line;
and animals flock to listen.

Musicians play tuneful notes;
they add their colorful harmonies,
to produce soulful renditions.

Life Is Precious

People leave imprints behind:
laughter, love, and actions.
They linger in minds forever.

Give support to people:
speech, deeds, and looks.
Love develops from these.

Disease makes one think
whether artistic works
will last despite snags.

Smile each day to beings.
The end may be not far,
to give help to humans.

Time Passes

As children, time moves fast.
Our leisure may zip past.
A minute moves in a blast,
and years provide problems.

As seniors, vigor's less,
but pleas are high from groups.
If you work with no mess,
you'll find there's less to clean.

If people watched your times,
they'd know the jobs you do.
They'd pay you extra dimes,
and see your point of view.

Do what you can do,
but don't do all that's asked;
for you will get quite blue,
if you listen to rumors.

I'm Thankful for...

I'm Thankful for . . .

sunny days this year.
joyous and cheery comments.
varied kinds of food.

lime and cerise food.
having distinct tastes.
different kinds of flavors.

a cozy bed for rest.
cold and humid nights.
freedoms people enjoy.

a time for labor or rest.
a chance to pursue dreams.
a time for loving acts.

God's Word to study.
prayers to Him daily.
a prepared, heavenly home.

Decisions

What should I do?
The question comes
in work or play.
And when I work,
what job comes first?

One strives to live,
and do their chores,
but sorting out
another's life
becomes futile.

Debates take time
to ponder and sort,
the work one aims
to do each day.
The methods matter.

When should one
no longer drive
for self-protection?
Should a dwelling
be sold for safety?

Discernment takes
some time to decide.
A person must choose
what's best for them,
for some balance.

Connections

I recollect the rituals of college life: courses, chapel,
and professors. The syllabi, sundry and demanding, I cram
in books.

My dorm room holds book piles, tossed in such disarray,
of Homer, Huxley, Hemingway, and Joyce with notes inside.
Those literary treasures, unlike books of youth, adorn
my antique table, twin bed, and wooden floor. A gooseneck
lamp, twists up and down, and from left to right; it burns
brightly in the midnight hours. In the pink light of day,
I scramble for my things. I throw on clothes, wrinkled from
   a cramped space.

In haste, I buy a cinnamon bun and whole, white milk.
While juggling my books and instant breakfast, I place
   delicious food
in my mouth. The bell sounds loudly; it sends me on my way.
I listen as the thoughts spew forth from scholars and
   the masters.
My pen, I press tightly in my hand, flows at stock
   car speeds.
The lectures last from half past eight until noon, and
there's still homework to do. Sometimes, I set aside
school clothes; I don formalwear or shorts.
For spontaneous events, I sit in pajamas.

Attire for rare, blind dates consist of a dress, heels, stockings,
and a makeup mask. I never know what I might need:
a looking glass or blindness.

Memories

Souvenir reminders of yesteryear
rest in storage, along with diplomas of old.
Keepsakes show records and interests of before.

Thank-you notes, from children, stay hidden from view,
which display sincerity and love, despite mistakes:
spelling, syntax, grammar, or punctuation.

Youth grow older and responsibilities change:
parents, a spouse, employees, a home, and pets.
Moms appreciate reminders of caring.

Ms. Kim

There is a doll on Brown Street,
who seldom is at home.
She goes places with Nancy,
and rests on the silty loam.

Nancy plays in the sun,
and takes her things in and out,
to enjoy the bright outside,
in her choice place to hangout.

The doll gets dirty with stains
from frequent visits, outside;
her reddish-brown hair has mats,
from many times cast aside.

Once Kim returns to the room,
her stay isn't long this time;
for the doll goes in the trash,
because of all the grime.

That night when Nancy rests,
she looks for Kim's special place.
Nancy searches each cranny,
but cannot find Kim's face.

The tears appear on Nancy,
and outside it's getting dim.
Her mother has a new doll,
but Nancy wants just Ms. Kim.

Then Nancy's mother digs deep
into the garbage pail,
to find the dirty doll,
and Nancy will not wail.

With Mother's tender hands,
the doll is like new.
Mom provides the right touch;
she puts the doll in view.

Time Moves On

People work hard to get things done;
leisure time is not used wisely.
Time goes slowly when we're young;
through the decades, the clock gets sprung.

Seniors struggle with chores each day;
rings of the phone interfere.
Strangers ask with voices sincere
for money and time, we hold dear.

People say, "You don't do enough."
But if eyes watched you for a while,
people would see the things you do,
and become your positive glue.

What's the answer to your dilemma?
Should you do less, so you don't burn
out as a sizzling and smoldering ember?
Will you become an active member

of the arts? Leave some tasks.
You'll have time to do some art,
and maybe you'll become extra stable.
Perhaps, you can try to write a fable.

Remembrances

Four decades of changes,
they're more than I see
on your arms and trunk,
and from a strained knee;

but your face is a light
of love, hope, and cheer.
I behold your beauty
because you're sincere.

The students dining
are multifarious.
A thread joins scholars
from the gregarious.

I connect with your warmth
on the night that we dined.
I seek more scholars;
they've left us behind.

The scholars not here
hold a special dream.
My mind has beliefs;
I behold each gleam.

Are marriages and births
receiving sentiments?
Are friends pushed for time?
They share not their laments.

Do lanterns shine brightly,
in places, far and near?
Do people have jobs,
to bring some extra cheer?

Chains of Sisterhood

Freshmen enter with helping hands
for the weaving to begin.
When homesickness sets in,
sisters soothe hearts and minds with time.

As honor and thanks to their junior sisters,
younger girls rise before the sun.
Garments go on; they're frocks for work.
No makeup goes on for outside chores.

Sisters gather huge, showy flowers,
while others gather shiny vines,
for the flower chain. Twisted chains
go on shoulders, like spring's trees.

Impressions

The teacher's career spans forty years;
the master questions her scholars' brains.
She motivates with four approaches:
lectures, questions, comments and wit.
Her lecture shows Shakespearean thought,
which resounds throughout the massive room.
Her linguistic style includes set values,
while she upholds specific traditions.

Her snowy, angelic hair shows off
her circular face. Her eyes support
the students' interests. Though petite in height,
she stands a giant among the thinkers;
she challenges students to look at their soul.
The teacher assists with her rhetorical style,
to leave with knowledge: an enduring legacy.

A Bolt from the Blue

The classic, reliable car
delivers a booming noise;
its visit for repairs confirms
car suspicions. Repairs
lead to uneasiness;
one ponders what to do.
Will the automobile
continue trips for chores?

The drives for Christmas shopping,
along with a Macon trip,
to see a younger sibling,
put more wear on the car.
A terrible noise sounds forth.
An engine light comes on;
it warns of coming trouble.
The car gets occupants home.

A belt's replacement might fix
it, becomes the sanguine dream,
until a phone call message
delivers the only options;
fix it, or trade it are choices.
A large repair payment
may be the start of others,
or monthly car loan payments.

A car sits on the pavement,
ready for reliable spins.

The Furor Dissipates

The driver's wrong turn creates a furor,
and slows down options for pain and relief.
Agitation mounts and develops.
The driver sits down in disbelief.

An inward desperation builds
with subtle hints becoming a tempest.
A dormant volcano awakens through faults;
it ascends and smolders inside the breast.

The driver spews frustrations and words,
until a traffic light shines ahead;
his anger subsides from gentle words.
The strife ceases; it leaves with more ease.

Encouragement in Life

Life, exists each day,
to work, study, and play;
living life changes us.
In an hour's fragments,
God can send the showers.

The sun bursts forth ahead,
from talking with Him, daily.
A quiet peace embraces.
His brilliance filters the rain;
friends' faces reflect the light.

Family circles surround;
encouragement flows around.
Loving strength sustains us.
Echoes resound from God:
"I'll never leave you alone."

Who Cares?

Does any person care
when your heart is beating fast,
from the work that's hard to bear,
and your mind thinks of the past?

Does any person care
when you've made a mistake?
Incidents seem not fair,
that life seems hard to take.

You race against the clock.
Does any human care?
You cannot darn a sock,
or have a minute to spare.

Is there one who cares that
a fever strikes your being?
Or, your nose has a bruise,
and eyes no longer are seeing?

Yes, there is one to care,
beyond the earth's measure.
Talk with Him, to share.
God's your greatest treasure.

A Silent Answer

Lord, I need some prayer,
for help through pain and grief.
You say, "My child I'll help
through all circumstances."
I pray, oh Lord, for mercy.
Your answer comes from grace.
But then the death call comes;
it leaves me unaware
of where to turn to You,
when Your perfect will's there.
Your name I call upon.
You furnish hope for now.
You promise endless life
through Your exaltation,
where tears no longer fall,
but love, jewels, and riches.
You provide such peace.

Musical Sounds

Music inspires my soul;
it rings within my ears.
The sound of the computer
starts my musical day.

The whir of the washer
is like a drum in my ear;
the motion going around
sends my head in a spin.

The noise of the mini radio
blasts pop and hip-hop,
before I turn the dial
to easy sounds of music.

The television resounds
within the boisterous house,
with stars delighting me.
Refrains stimulate.

The choristers of my church
give praises unto God;
their voices blend together,
to reach the lost souls.

Songs and steady beats
replay in my head;
the record doesn't stop;
it sounds within my bed.

Music at Night

The great music doesn't leave my head;
it bounces up and down and all around.
While sleeping, it resides with me in bed.
The notes slip in and out without a sound.

Some notes resound, and my throat opens wide;
then closes more for a rumbling sound.
And pitches swell like a foamy tide,
yet ebb and flow, near the sandy ground.

Pulses dance and resound in my brain;
a rhythm becomes offbeat.
I move along without any pain,
as hands and body move with my feet.

My eyes pop open to welcome the morn;
when through the window, I hear a loud horn.

Play the Ivories

"Come play me," the piano said.
"Play my ivories for a while.
Limber hands with arpeggios;
play those melodies for a time.
Entertain everyone.
Play simple pieces and complex;
recreate hymns, pop, or jazz.
Create tunes of fire and sadness.
Strike those keys, lightly and firmly.
Indulge yourself, on my device;
press ivories to make music."

Open Doors

Global events are set,
to showcase the arts;
they help establish bonds.

Foreign friendships help,
to improve relationships.
Diplomacy begins to come.

Ambassadors speak together;
they develop relationships
for foreign affairs to work.

Relationships are built in
science, sports, and music.
They initiate peace.

Choices

Daily, we have numerous choices to make;
we search for instant options to take.
The mind sorts through facts of each case,
with limitations, we might face.

One finds an answer by going slowly.
Answers are dependent on Him, wholly.
One ponders conditions, far and near,
to get the right advice, from a dear.

We have a choice of a decision;
we search our voice, without derision.
God imparts words to us in His love,
on the wings of a simple dove.

When the Sun Rises

The dawn of the day arises;
the light declares, "Get going.
Make the bright day count;
leave behind the darkness."

"Rise from your comfortable mattress,
and cast aside your comforter,
along with dreams or visions;
replace with actual ambitions."

"Step in front of duties.
Fuel the body with food
to nourish you through the day.
So, you move upward in life."

"For God's effulgence adds warmth;
His light supplies a beginning
to enhance some creativity,
and one can revel in assignments."

Music

Rhythmic and delightful,
expands creative genius,
lifts the spirit:
melody.

Fleeing from the Enemy

God, help me with decisions;
my options are unclear,
as I walk here to work.
I'm vulnerable in my gait,
as I plan options to take,
for tasks become protracted.
Discernment takes my trust,
while fleeing enemy darts.

Your shelter shields from the storms:
a refuge for communing.
I'll extol Your name forever.
I seek Your open arms,
to blot out my transgressions.
You alone give peace,
after the enemy leaves.
You restore the spirit.

When I fall short of conditions,
You accept my flaws.

Wishes

Displays can capture eyes
to lure you in as fish.
The search for granting wishes
makes the giver weigh things:
the disposition, the use,
and the cost of the gift.

Personalities consist:
the doer, the homebody,
and the collector. For people at home,
the giver presents slipper
socks, with nonskid bottoms,
pajamas, or lounge clothes.

The doer delights in gear:
gardening, yard work, or sports.
The gift card is unlike
all garments or gadgets there.
For receivers, can share in gifts:
the when and how of wishes.

Live in the Moment

Dear Lord, today, I'll sweep the dirt from my house.
I'll sweep the webs from my head, which contain things,
that don't help me be productive: worker and follower.
You know it's easy, Lord, to bog down with tasks
to worry about: family, finances, and jobs.

Once I'm awake, I'll enlist Your help; for You
know the directions I'm pulled towards with tasks.
I'll spend time communing with You: prayer and Scripture.
My mind can focus on jobs to complete. Then, I'll
sweep the distractions away from my life.

I'll praise and thank You for what You've done for me.
I'll enlist Your help; we'll be a winning team.
You never fail to keep Your awesome promises.

The Brain

The media express ideas, daily,
with their sources: Internet, papers,
newsletters, and magazines.
Food for thought these may be,
but represent rehashes of things.

Devices provide entertainment,
while stirring the listener with dialogue,
music, or images; they can't compete
with something else for the brain:
a new book to read and relax with.

Ideas expressed in books, though not new,
come in flavors: fiction, poetry,
and nonfiction. Subjects provide
components: structure, vocabulary,
plot, setting, characters, and events.

New books aid the process of thinking about
thinking. By modifying the thinking
structure, a reader can change erroneous
beliefs, expand topic knowledge, and
learn techniques for a book's composition.

Fans

Fans turn out for many events;
baseball and football bring the gents.
Football fans don't tire of the game,
but women see sports as the same.

Readers are fans of varied books,
and writers reel readers with their hooks.
They're trying to whet appetites,
through sketches of villains or knights.

Fans of music like various kinds;
musicians compose: they're masterminds.
Whether one listens to jazz or pop,
people move with pizzazz and a hop.

One's pursuits may lead to careers,
or be fun till retirement nears.
One needs escape from severe strain,
to help one keep a healthy brain.

Fans in our world do work and play.
So, living is not about one's pay.   .
Each fan has a purpose to set the stage,
for how each human does at any age.

The Missing Phone

Where has the phone gone?
I hear no dial tone.

Is it hiding in the house?
Is it clinging as a louse,

on my bird or tiny dog,
that sits in mud, like a hog?

Will the phone appear again?
It's not in the dog's wire pen.

I press a button on the base,
to hear where it has given chase.

I listen for the deafening tone;
it's muted notes sound like a groan.

A ringing sound comes from the bed.
I lift apparel, where it's fled.

Laughter

When laughter fills the air,
we start to look for the source.
Does it come from a well
of happiness from within?

Episodic relief
provides release from stress.
Silly creature antics
bring leaps of joy out.

One's crazy styles and clothes
present times to chuckle.
Necklines that plunge
may be unattractive.

Skirts can be so skimpy;
they show unmentionables.
Slips edge below hems,
causing humiliation.

Moments lead to chuckles.
Minds, not working right,
make eating trips at night.
We forget why we are going.

Political speeches we hear,
strike some comical notes,
when candidates promise
what will be forgotten soon.

Laughter adds years to life.
So, we seek laughs today,
to make our day complete,
for fun along the way.

Aids for a Life

Planning aids help us live:
notes and notepads.
They serve as reminders daily
of appointments and major dates.

Reminders keep lives on track,
so not much comes in a day,
a week, or a month. We live,
not as a race of events.

People run to events;
it makes them less productive.
Time must exist to plan.
Bodies need rests or breaks;

they must have leisure.
One can rest by reading.
Help to others is important,
but one must rest for patience.

Daily Vigor

Strength of body, mind, and soul
comes from where to face life's snags?
People have hurdles every day,

whether hard or simple problems.
Problem solving takes time and effort.
We pray and work to pull us through.

God will lead you and give you grace,
while you carry out tasks to do.
Take some time for energy breaks,

to keep from feeling tired and swamped.
Try to live one day at a time.
You will have persistence and patience.

A Myriad of People

In the cool and gray of the morning, vendors
use colored tents for setting out wares.
Tables support the wares and food;
large signs and yard chairs complete the booths.

Jewelry, books, and games grab eyes.
People look for special gifts
for playful and unusual things,
not often found in shops or stores.

Children run and jump and spin,
in rectangular, inflated, and jumpable enclosures,
or in shade and open areas.
Animal balloons hang from arms;

they wait for hands to connect with them.
The antique cars have metal grills,
and rumble seats for tiny passengers.
The eyes of passersby can see.

All ages revel in the day's events:
shopping, playing, eating and visiting.
The summer's cool mornings give way, soon,
to nature's sweltering heat: the sun.

Images

Mirrors present the images,
faces of blue eyes with lines,
filled with long ringlets of hair;
the hair falls to the shoulders.

Faces are round and chubby;
short-bob hair frames the face.
Light azure eyes poke out.
Beings may view weathered years.

Emotions exude from the mouth;
a rubber band smile stretches out.
The smile forms a sourish lemon;
it stretches again to a smile.

For writers spill out their words;
they lock in desirable remarks.
Readers see the images
of contextual meaning or plot.

Characters tangle in webs;
they work out unique solutions,
to move each story along,
and tie up the missing pieces.

A Peaceful Stroll

While walking by a stony path,
a squirrel I chanced to meet.
He clutched an acorn in front paws
and hunched on his back feet.
He sat quite still as I approached
until he saw me near.
Then with a dash he ran away
and headed towards the sky.

In a flash, tree branches shook,
as he squirmed and danced above.
His bunchy tail shook the green leaves
and bounced around as he fled.
The leafy path that lined my way
welcomed me with an arm.
The trees stretched out to draw me in,
and green ferns added charm.

The path was lined with profiles of trees,
along this tranquil place,
where nature's voices and lovely sights
made me walk at a slow pace.
The serene sounds and appealing sights
brought enchantment to my soul,
and the brush of the wind upon my face
ended my peaceful stroll.

Things That Count

How long does it take to say you care,
to offer a gift of a thing so rare?

It doesn't take much time at all,
to write a note, or place a call.

Attentive ears can fill a need;
they give wisdom one may heed.

The time you spend in one's life
can help them deal with inner strife.

A thoughtful word becomes a ray
of hope to help one today.

Will you carry out God's plan,
to love and serve your fellow man?

Acknowledgments

A big thank you goes to all the writers in my groups for their help. Without your encouragement, it would be impossible to do the writing. I have friends on the social sites that give me support, too. My husband, Charles Cruzan, helps with many chores, so I'm able to get my books out. I'm thankful that we met.

Another big thank you goes to Pam Mulhern for editing some of the poetry. I appreciate Charlotte Norton's encouragement. I appreciate the cards, the food, the gifts, and the visits during my recent surgery. I appreciate all the time and effort.

About the Author

Patricia Cruzan writes poetry. Her articles, stories, and poems are in various publications. The latest poetry book is her third collection. The poetry books include *Poetic Moments, My Reflections*, and *Sketches of Life*.

She is the author of four children's books. The titles of the books are *The Wonder in the Woods, Max Does It Again, Molly's Mischievous Dog*, and *Tall Tales of the United States*. An untitled book will be coming out later.

Patricia is a member of Georgia Writers Association, Writers Circle, Poet Tree, SCBWI, and SPAWN. Previously, she taught in Georgia, Texas, and Louisiana.

www.ingramcontent.com/pod-product-compliance
Lightning Source LLC
LaVergne TN
LVHW051602080426
835510LV00020B/3102